You are not alone!

Julie Barnhill ☺

You are not alone!
Julie Barrow

Every
Mother
Can Beat
the Blues

Every Mother Can Beat the Blues

Julie Barnhill

a division of Baker Publishing Group
Grand Rapids, Michigan

© 2008 by Julie Barnhill

Published by Revell
a division of Baker Publishing Group
P.O. Box 6287, Grand Rapids, MI 49516-6287
www.revellbooks.com

Printed in the United States of America

All rights reserved. No part of this publication may be reproduced, stored in a retrieval system, or transmitted in any form or by any means—for example, electronic, photocopy, recording—without the prior written permission of the publisher. The only exception is brief quotations in printed reviews.

ISBN 978-0-8007-1899-2

Unless otherwise indicated, Scripture is taken from the HOLY BIBLE, NEW INTERNATIONAL VERSION®. NIV®. Copyright © 1973, 1978, 1984 by International Bible Society. Used by permission of Zondervan. All rights reserved.

Scripture quotations marked Message are taken from *The Message* by Eugene H. Peterson, copyright © 1993, 1994, 1995, 2000, 2001, 2002. Used by permission of NavPress Publishing Group. All rights reserved.

Published in association with the literary agencies of Alive Communications, Inc., 7680 Goddard Street, Suite 200, Colorado Springs, Colorado 80920, and Fedd & Company, Inc., 9759 Concord Pass, Brentwood, Tennessee 37027.

As women, we hold within our grasp
the power to change the world.

One family at a time.

One mother heart at a time.

We **don't** have to run for political office.
We **don't** have to write books.
We **don't** have to tell a hundred thousand people the details of our journey.

No,

we can make all the difference

simply

by telling the truth of our life.

To ourselves first . . . then to **one another**.

Do you find yourself feeling

blue,

downcast,

gloomy,

dispirited,

low,
pushed down,

isolated,

sad,

discouraged,

flat,

empty,

numb,

weary,
dejected,
heavyhearted

- and dealing with depression?

Just between you and me—each word of experience, prayer, insight, gentle warning, and real-life proof of lasting change mentioned within these pages was first tested and lived out (for better or worse) in my own family relationships as a mom.

You are not alone. Thousands upon thousands of women have shared with me personally via conversation, email, phone calls, or handwritten letters that, yes, even tough mothers struggle with getting the blues, stress, anger, and fleeting humor reserves.

The truth is, it isn't so much about getting everything right. Who among us reading these pages could honestly claim to have done that as a mother anyway? The important thing is acknowledging specific matters in our life as a mom for which we desperately need and desire change. And I can't think of anyone more willing and able to step up and do just that than me. So relax and stay awhile as we take a closer look at depression and discover inspirational and practical tools to deal with it.

Few friends and relatives would have ever pegged me for depression during my late twenties and early thirties. After all, I was the gregarious young wife of a kind and devoted husband, Rick, who was crazy about me and truly appreciated my rounder, fuller, post-babies shape. I was

> the mother of three adorable children,
>
> the beloved adopted daughter of a warm and nurturing mother and father,
>
> a passionate leader of Bible studies in my home and church,
>
> and an aspiring "I'm going to make my dream happen" author and speaker.

Every Mother Can Beat the Blues

By all outward appearances my life was

sweet,

simple,

and easy.

So what was the deal with my sleeping twelve-plus hours yet never feeling rested? I slept when the baby slept and enforced mandatory "rest time" for the older two children. Once the older two started preschool and kindergarten, I would often take my youngest to a nearby sitter (wonderful, amazing Karla Jones) and then return home and sleep for an additional two to four hours. Waking just before I needed to pick the children up at school, I would madly dash through the house—picking up this, putting away that—to prove to myself (and Rick) that I had actually accomplished something during the day.

What was the deal with the debilitating fatigue rendering me fuzzy, lethargic, disjointed, and disinterested in nearly all mental, physical, spiritual, and sexual aspects of my still-young life?

And what, pray tell, one afternoon in the middle of an otherwise sunny and beautiful spring day, was the terrifying deal with the "this-close-to-suicidal" thoughts I had while lying in bed with a sheet and a down comforter pulled up to my eyes?

Maybe it had something to do with my spiritual life—it wasn't "good" enough.

No deal.

I was probably reading and studying the Bible more than I ever had in my married adult life. I was learning things and growing in my faith. I was leading those studies in my home, remember? My prayer life was strong. And I knew beyond a shadow of a doubt that writing and speaking was going to be a reality a little bit farther down the road.

Perhaps I wasn't exercising enough.
Hmm, let me rephrase that.
Perhaps I wasn't exercising at all, and maybe that had something to do with my weight.

Deal, begrudgingly so.

This thing with actually moving my body for anything unrelated to shoe shopping, browsing through bookstores, or getting to the other side of the house, well, it never really seemed all that important or interesting to me. However, once I saw a rising number display each time I stepped on my scale, well, that did get my attention. But honestly, I never saw the purpose nor felt the need for sweating and heavy breathing, except for great sex!

Maybe I was *the* poster child for the Worst Kind of Christian.

No deal!

And don't you dare pick up what other people would drop regarding this either. Depression isn't some psycho, non-Christian disease, for crying out loud! It's a complex mental disorder caused by varying factors. Yes, the spiritual element of our creation comes into play—it couldn't possibly be divorced from how we feel—but our struggle with the blues is not a flashing neon faith indicator of how far we've missed the mark.

**Perhaps it had
a lot to do with little things.**

Deal—blissfully sane and truthful deal.

Our lives are filled with emotional, spiritual, mental, financial, and physical complexities. Our bodies as well as our relationships are pieced together with nuanced details. For many it's not so much one big thing as it is a maddening plethora of small things that contribute to our depression.

That black dog.
—Winston Churchill

*Spending all day in bed
and still not getting a good night's rest.*
—Anonymous

depre

. . . a plain and simple
reduction of feeling.

—Judith Guest

The inability to
construct a future.
—*Rollo May*

ssion

It is what it is . . .

I wish something would again matter.
—Allan G.

A state of feeling sad.
—Merriam-Webster online dictionary

Depression is a reality for 1 out of 8 women during her lifetime.

Next time you're out in public or driving along in your car, take a moment and scan the number of females around you—count off: 1, 2, 3, 4, 5, 6, 7, **8**—one of them will struggle with the blues in her lifetime; (keep counting) 9, 10, 11, 12, 13, 14, 15, **16**—one of them will join the ranks of 12 million women in the United States experiencing clinical depression; (keep counting and practicing your multiples of 8s) 17, 18, 19, 20, 21, 22, 23, **24** ...

Indeed, you are not alone!

Depression is a real and serious condition that can impact every area of life.

Socially what used to be easy and relaxing to do, like running around with girlfriends, hosting family and friends for dinner, or simply going to the grocery store, becomes taxing—something to dread and avoid. And the simple conversations most people take for granted? Bantering with salesclerks? Engaging that sweet old lady sitting next to you for the next four hours on your flight home? Well, there's no such thing as simple anything in the social realm when it comes to depression.

Sexually what used to be easy, pleasurable, and desirable to do and achieve, like foreplay, intercourse, the big "O," becomes taxing—something to dread and avoid. Adding to the depression is realizing how insidiously and gradually this once integral part of our life can drop off the radar screen of our thoughts, our body, our desire. One day, *poof,* it's gone.

Self-worth and purpose, not surprisingly, take a huge hit. If you are unable, literally unable, to *do* what you used to do physically or sexually, or to *be* mentally, intellectually, and spiritually all that has defined you as a woman and given you perceived value, is it any wonder you find yourself crippled with insecurity and doubt?

Depression is highly treatable with a combination of healthy lifestyle habits, medicinal grace, and wise therapeutic counsel.

There's an undeniable link between physical and mental health. Making healthy choices can dramatically improve your mood: regular exercise, healthy sleep habits (some of you may want to speak with your family doctor and investigate possible sleep apnea issues if severe sleepiness during the daytime is a problem), daily sunlight (just getting yourself out the door can be difficult, but those few minutes of sunshine can work wonders on the body, mood, and mind), a nutritious diet (hmm, I'm going to stay very quiet on this particular topic), and avoiding alcohol and drugs (sometimes difficult to do when they beckon as a form of escape and relief).

Antidepressants. I grieve that some critics consider antidepressants a crutch. More grievous still are people of faith who slap an "un-Christian" tag on a person's struggle with the blues and depression.

> Here's truth: just as God—the Creator of the ends of the earth—demonstrated divine grace to us by revealing Himself through Jesus,
> so too, the Creator of every nuanced facet of your body, mind, and soul
> demonstrates and provides "medicinal grace"
> through the intellectual knowledge of doctors, pharmacists, and counselors.
> May we never scoff at such grace—for ourselves or those around us!

Consider the complexities of our bodies: estrogen raging and ebbing—hormonal fluctuations during our menstrual cycle or its frustratingly sporadic appearance. We bloat. We're irritable. And yes, on occasion we respond emotionally. In light of these realities of our creation and day-to-day realities, may we never discount the jaw-dropping complexities of who we are and how we are put together! May we never diminish the kind grace of a Creator who gifts others to help us in our time of need.

Depression. It is what it is.

And it's not what it's not . . .

Depression is *not* something to be ashamed of.

Hear me on this: over the course of my life I've had to admit to actions and choices that fell smack-dab into the "I am ashamed" circle of life. But admitting I couldn't control the blues and seeking help for depression? Not one iota of shame there. I'm proud of you for facing it and moving forward in a manner that will help.

Depression is *not* "all in your mind."

Depression is a disorder of the body as much as of the mind. Increasingly, there is evidence that depression involves multiple body systems. Your personal experience with depression can be as incredibly complex as you are and can stem from psychological, physiological, or spiritual dimensions.

Depression is *not* a sure sign of failure as a mother.

Oh, this one is much harder to believe, isn't it? After all, many of us believe mothers are supposed to be "strong" and "together" and a million other adjectives that mean "successful," right? Hear me on this: admitting our need for help, counsel, or guidance as a woman and mother *never* means we have failed. Indeed, it is one of the surest indicators of your strength.

Depression is *not* always easy to diagnose.

I spent three years going to doctors and counselors before anyone suggested the role depression might be playing in my life. Three years! Let me encourage you to ask as many questions as it takes, research as many symptoms as you need, and seek out wise counsel from doctors and therapists to diagnose the specifics of your struggle.

Depression is *not* the result of praying too little or not having enough faith (and who gets to make that call anyway?).

I am grateful to God that I have known the despair and loneliness of depression—especially during the months and years that observers of my life could have easily called the most successful spiritually. God requires of us but two things, mothers: to come to Him with the audacious trust and nature of a child—think of a toddler—and to ask anything and everything of Him with that toddler-like faith.

Perhaps some of you reading these pages have a picture of a grumpy god or a capricious god, listening and dismissing our cries for help and rescue. Let me assure you, this God is the God of the brokenhearted and the downcast, standing ready to heal and comfort (Psalm 147:3)! Keep on praying, knowing that He hears each and every prayer. Keep crying out (literally) and know your tears are stored and treasured by the one able to heal and restore (Psalm 56:8).

And now I'm flat on my face
  feeling sorry for myself morning to night.
All my insides are on fire,
  my body is a wreck.
I'm on my last legs; I've had it—
  my life is a vomit of groans.

Psalm 38:7-8 Message

Rick and I got married; went on our honeymoon; had a baby, Kristen, less than a year later; and moved due to his employment three states and twelve hours away from friends and family. While living so far from home, Rick sustained crippling injuries to his right knee and foot in a head-on car collision and was unable to work for six months.

During his time at home recovering and doing physical therapy, we racked up credit card debt due to expenses not covered by our insurance, as well as my panic shopping just to "deal" with my worry about Rick, his future health, and our ability to make it on two-thirds of his already stretched-to-the-limit paycheck.

Six months after his wreck, he was transferred back to our home state of Illinois, where we found a tiny house to rent. Twenty months after Kristen was born, I gave birth to her brother Ricky.

When our second child was born, we needed a larger home. We found one to rent and moved a week or so after his birth. And yes, that's two major moves across state lines and tearing down and setting up two different homes in less than a year's time.

Look for more discussion about stress and its impact in our lives as mothers in the book *Every Mother Can Let Go of Stress.*

During the next couple of years, my birth mother and I, with whom I had made contact during my senior year of college, were unable to create and maintain a healthy relationship. Perhaps it's more accurate to say that I didn't have the slightest clue how to deal with all the emotions caused by her limited presence in my life.

(*Sigh.*) It's pretty convoluted, as are many of the details of any life. Suffice it to say there were innumerable other experiences that were part of our floundering relationship that confused me and caused great heartache.

A few more years and I gave birth to my third child, Patrick, who was diagnosed at six weeks with sleep apnea. We learned this after witnessing a terrifying moment of his desperately trying to wake up and start breathing during a catnap. Had he not been lying in his sister's arms and her crying out in fear, we may not have noticed the ashen gray pallor of his skin and the indescribably murky focus of his eyes.

For the next fifteen months, Patrick was tethered to a life-saving apnea monitor, which released a piercingly pitched shrill warning all but declaring: "He's not breathing! He's not breathing!" Each time it happened, it felt like shock waves running through my body.

Trust me, there was little rest or peace in our home during those many months.

And as I look back, I can't help but shake my head and try somehow retroactively to comfort the fragile, confused, and sad young mother I was those many years ago. I would reassure her and say, "Given the complexities of your circumstances, it's no wonder you couldn't keep it all together. It's no wonder you fell apart."

So too with you, my friend.

Your life is incredibly complex.

Maddeningly so.

Yet you can't really see that. Probably you can't appreciate the stresses of your life, for you are, in all likelihood, too busy beating yourself up for not doing "more" or doing "better" or any number of the graceless things we tell ourselves. But hear me: it is what it is—the blues, depression, and life. God will never abandon or forget you as a result of your humanness and the way you deal with the multiple stressors in your life.

Lord God,

so many times I not only feel, but am, overwhelmed with the concerns of being

> a mother, a wife, a daughter, a friend, and a believer.

I wake up and before my feet hit the floor my mind is racing, my breath shallow, as mentally I list the seemingly unending responsibilities of the day ahead.

> *It terrifies me many times.*
>
> > I wonder how on earth I'll get through another day.

I'm tired.

I've lost the energy that once propelled me through the rough spots.

> > Yet everyone is depending on me.

Do You see me, Lord?

Do You care?

It's hard to know—difficult to feel Your presence. And I so desperately need to feel something—anything—other than this blank, dull sense of nothingness.

My faith?

Well, it is small.
Probably not even close to the size of a mustard seed—but I give it to You anyway.

I have no other choice.

For I know You are Life.

Self-Care
to Help You Cope and Heal

Find someone to talk to about your feelings.

There will be times when you are the lifeline for another mother.

You will be the saving grace for her children.

And you will be the reason that mother is able to believe she truly isn't alone.

Accept offers for help

with child care, housework, and errand running. Swallow any "I should be able to do this myself" pride and allow others to bless you and your family.

And rest and sleep.

Do something *relaxing* —every day.

Give credit where credit is due!

You got a shower in before 9:00 pm—pat yourself on your good-smelling shoulder.

You returned two emails and one voice message—one more than you did the week before. That's progress.

You held your baby and gave thanks for his or her creation—this is love.

Speak truth:

> "No one expects me to be Super Mom—
> *except me, perhaps.*"

Speak more truth:

> "I cannot be Super Mom,
> and I won't beat myself up for it."

If you're finding it difficult to differentiate your symptoms or sort through the myriad of feelings after childbirth, after a miscarriage, or while making your way through everyday life, please consult your physician. You can't always "fix" yourself, and oftentimes the best decision involves admitting you need an outside opinion and wise counsel. It's that medicinal grace thing I wrote about on pages 31–32, remember?

In-between said doctor's appointment and the current "here and now," keep reading and take the time to answer the following questions, homing in on your current state of mind over the past two weeks. Consider the following entries from my journal and the specific follow-up statements to be an unofficial "real mother" screening test of sorts.

These questions should not replace in any way, shape, or form a more formal evaluation with a trusted physician. Let them be what they're intended to be: a safe spot to admit to sometimes confusing, overwhelming, or embarrassing emotions. Use your answers to jumpstart a conversation with your doctor regarding your thoughts and feelings at this time.

Answer honestly and be unafraid to seek help if needed.

Another day of sunshine and the sun warming my skin, but inside I feel dull ... gray ... flat. Flat is the best word. Like I'm watching the kids play but I'm a million miles away. It takes all my mental energy just to be present emotionally and relationally. And I'm worn out from the effort. What's wrong with me, and how long is this going to last?

Over the past two weeks, I have looked forward with enjoyment to things (activities, time with children, etc.).

☐ Not at all ☐ More than half the days
☐ Several days ☐ Nearly every day

Over the past two weeks, I have been able to laugh and enjoy the funny side of life.

☐ Not at all ☐ More than half the days
☐ Several days ☐ Nearly every day

Is there anything that doesn't seem to set my panic alarm on full blast? Forgotten homework assignments shoved in my face to be signed on the way to school—panic! Television reporters informing me about some sort of early morning bad news—panic! But I'm the mom. I'm the one who's supposed to have it all together. Yet, there are days and weeks when it feels like one more piece of the jigsaw puzzle called "My Life" comes up missing.

Over the past two weeks, I have felt scared or panicky for no good reason.

☐ Not at all   ☐ More than half the days
☐ Several days   ☐ Nearly every day

Over the past two weeks, experiences in my life have been too much for me.

☐ Not at all   ☐ More than half the days
☐ Several days   ☐ Nearly every day

This is not the real me. And that's the truth I keep telling myself as I meet with my counselor, take my medication, and literally cry out to God while slogging incrementally forward hour by hour, day by day, week by week. Feelings—debilitating feelings of dejection and spiritual/emotional fatigue are beginning to fade as hope takes root in my soul and mind. I never realized how much I missed its presence!

Over the past two weeks, I have been so unhappy that I have had difficulty sleeping.

☐ Not at all ☐ More than half the days
☐ Several days ☐ Nearly every day

Over the past two weeks, I've had a poor appetite or indulged in overeating.

☐ Not at all ☐ More than half the days
☐ Several days ☐ Nearly every day

Over the past two weeks, I have been so unhappy that I have been crying.

☐ Not at all ☐ More than half the days
☐ Several days ☐ Nearly every day

Over the past two weeks, the thought of harming myself has occurred to me.

☐ Not at all ☐ More than half the days
☐ Several days ☐ Nearly every day

My overall ability to feel, function, and/or perform emotionally, relationally, sexually, and spiritually has been affected.

☐ Not at all ☐ Moderately
☐ Mildly ☐ Severely

I had an epiphany while typing those questions. Then again, it was more of a flashback—an enlightening flashback!

Around the third question, I began to think, *These words sure sound familiar*, and my memory went back to about 1996. I was sitting in the austere counseling room of the lone psychotherapist whose services were covered by my husband's insurance plan.

Anyway, my mind went back to that day and I realized those were the exact questions the doctor had asked during my post–third-child period, and "I'm in here for some serious help with my depression" visit. But he didn't ask the questions in any manner whatsoever that would win my trust or honest response.

In fact, when I walked in and sat down, the first thing he did was pull down a gargantuan mental health manual with multiple Post-it notes for bookmarks and begin flipping Post-it to Post-it.

Every Mother Can Beat the Blues

Dr.: "In the past seven days, have you been anxious or worried for no good reason?"

Me: Uh, yes.

Dr.: (*turns the page*) "In the past seven days have you felt sad or miserable?"

Me: Uh, sorta.

Dr.: (*turns the page and maintains zero eye contact with the self-confessed anxious, worried, sad, or miserable client*) "In the past seven days have you thought of harming yourself or believed the world would be a better place without you in it?" (*blink*).

Dr.: (*turns the pa . . . . . .*

Are you kidding me?

Did he honestly think he could ask such antiseptic questions and get by with it? Had other clients allowed him to slide by with such inept chair-side manner?

Well, I may have been anxious, worried, sad, and/or miserable, but something snarky sparked within me and, after an awkward minute or two of silence, I looked him in the eye and replied to his third and final question.

> Me: "Have I thought of harming myself or believed the world would be a better place without me? No, not really"* (long uncomfortable pause). "But I have often thought the world would be a better place if some other people weren't in it."
>
> Dr.: (madly scribbling *my committal papers*)

---

*Which wasn't entirely true for I had thought that very thing a matter of days before.

Depression Dos and Don'ts

Countless women like me have learned the right and not-so-right ways to go about handling the blues and depression. I encourage you to learn from our experiences as you move forward confidently and take a proactive approach to your health: mentally, emotionally, and spiritually.

Do look for and demand a doctor with whom you are absolutely comfortable, one who respects and holds in highest regard warm and personal interaction. This is not the time for cold and indifferent help!

Every Mother Can Beat the Blues

Don't blame yourself for your depression—clinical or postpartum.

Do research and look for the best medicinal options if you are breastfeeding; this may require alternative options to pharmaceuticals—homeopathic treatments with the consent of your primary physician, relaxation methods, light exercise, healthier food choices, more sleep.

Don't be discouraged for not feeling better sooner or faster than you expected. Be patient. Getting over the blues and making your way out of depression take time. Depression is treatable, and you can have great success if you'll allow others to come alongside you.

Do call your doctor or the local suicide center if you have thoughts of taking your life or the life of your child.

Don't underestimate the power of crisis counseling.

Many mothers have "unspeakable feelings" about their children and themselves; however, if you find yourself struggling with homicidal urges, pick up the phone and speak with a professional crisis counselor immediately at 1-800-4-A-CHILD.

If you fear you might take your own life, you can speak with a trained counselor twenty-four hours a day at 1-800-273-TALK (8255) and be routed to the closest possible crisis center in your area.

Lord,

It's good to know I'm not alone.

Good to know

—no, liberating to know—

my depression does not have to define
who I am.

It's what I struggle with—not who I am.
Give me understanding to discern the dynamics of this struggle.

Lead me to the best doctor and counselor who will effectively and wisely help me get a leash on and no longer be led by the "black dog."

Show me **truth**.

Expose any lies that I have believed about myself,

You,

my children,

or this illness,

which are contributing to its presence.

Help me, God. Help me!

Do keep on keeping on.

Persistence.

Nothing in the world can take the place of persistence.

Talent will not; nothing is more common than unsuccessful men with talent.

Genius will not; unrewarded genius is almost a proverb.

Education will not; the world is full of educated derelicts.

Persistence and determination alone are omnipotent.

The slogan, "Press on," has solved and always will solve the problems of the human race.

Calvin Coolidge

You've got to work with what you've got and start where you are.

How's that for profound?

Okay, not so much maybe, but one of the keys to beating the blues is to start right here, right now, with whatever resources and energy you have. So, if your legs are in working order and as long as no dangerous weather impedes you, put down this book immediately, go outside, and take a walk around your house or apartment building. Or take the steps down a floor or two and then walk back—but if at all possible, get yourself outside and simply walk.

Take in the sights and sounds around you.

Pay close attention to the sky above you—day or evening.

And when you feel you've gone as far as you can possibly go—go one step farther.

Go on, what are you waiting for? Shoo! Go walk. I'll be here waiting for you when you get back.

I can do everything through him who gives me strength.

Philippians 4:13

Step-by-Step

> Take the first step, no more, no less,
> and the next will be revealed.
>
> —*Ken Roberts*

Consider the things you can do, or actions you have taken in the past, to relieve your depression. Choose one and do it—think it—pray it—believe it—change it—or share it. Take action and implement these ideas each and every day—when you're feeling depressed and even when you're feeling good.

Talk to a supportive friend. We were made for relationship, ladies, and I believe some of my strongest strides in growing healthy and breaking free from the grip of depression came as a result of old-fashioned girl talk.

Talk to Jesus—oh, now, don't roll your eyes or dismiss this too quickly out of hand. I'm reminded of something Beth Moore said during one of her video teaching sessions. Here it is via Julie paraphrase: "Your friends can and may get tired of hearing about your 'stuff.' But Jesus never grows tired of the length or the width or the depth of your need."

Give ear to my words, O Lord,
consider my sighing.
Listen to my cry for help,
my King and my God,
for to you I pray.
In the morning, O Lord, you hear
my voice;
in the morning I lay my re-
quests before you
and wait in expectation.

Psalm 5:1–3

This is the confidence we have
in approaching God:
that if we ask anything according
to his will, he hears us.

1 John 5:14

List truth about who you are:

A beloved child of God

A mother who loves her children

A woman with unique talents

A believer in Christ

A woman created and pieced together by God

Read a good book. Even in my darkest moments, I refused to give up reading. I guess my stubbornness can work to my benefit at times after all. I read books that helped me escape—books that made me laugh (oh, how I needed to do that!)—and the Book that placed my thoughts on truth, no matter what my emotions and feelings were telling me about God and myself.

> I discovered an astonishing truth: God is attracted to weakness. He can't resist those who humbly and honestly admit how desperately they need Him.
>
> Jim Cymbala
> *Fresh Wind, Fresh Fire*

Listen to music and take a long, hot bath. Or perhaps a long, hot shower sounds more relaxing. Either way, pamper yourself and indulge in aromatic bath soaps . . . a lit candle perhaps . . . dimmed lighting . . . and the sound of little ones trying to get your attention from behind the closed and locked door. *Smile!*

Do something nice for someone else. Oh, dear. This wasn't exactly my first, second, or even thirty-third thought during the "black dog" weeks and months. But it's wise advice nevertheless. There's something intrinsically powerful when we step outside ourselves and serve another.

> Perhaps it's playing a board game with your child.
> Gathering fallen branches in your neighbor's yard.
> Buying a bouquet of daisies for that supportive friend.
> Baking a homemade loaf of bread for your mom or putting together a yummy batch of chocolate chip cookies for your famished teenagers.

Do you see what this means—

all these pioneers who blazed the way, all these veterans cheering us on?

It means we'd better get on with it.

Strip down, start running—and never quit!

No extra spiritual fat, no parasitic sins.

Keep your eyes on *Jesus*, who both began and finished this race we're in.

Study how he did it.
Because he never lost sight of where he was headed—that exhilarating finish in and with God—

he could put up with anything along the way:

cross, shame, whatever.

And now he's *there*, in the place
of honor, right alongside God.

When you find yourselves flagging
in your faith, go over that story again,

    item by item,

    that long litany of hostility
    he plowed through.

That will shoot adrenaline into your
souls!

Hebrews 12:1-3 Message

Perhaps the cover of this book caught your eye on a Store-Mart shelf, grocery store kiosk, or library display. Maybe a mothers' group or book club you participate in chose it as their monthly pick, or you found it lying beneath a pile of reference materials in your physician's waiting room. Perhaps someone purchased it *for* you and/or recommended it *to* you and, given the title, you're just not quite sure what to think. Or perhaps you simply picked it up because it aptly describes where you have been or the place in which you currently find yourself as a mom.

No matter the path that brought you here, I'm so glad you came.

I tried my best to create a quick-to-read layout, easy to digest and easy to go to as a reference point in time(s) of need. I included all sorts of quotable quotes that you can tuck away in your memory and use as encouragement for yourself and others, as well as truth found in the Bible.

You see, this one thing I know to be true: change— true and lasting change for our weaknesses, failings, weariness, and worries—can and will ultimately come as the result of truth penetrating our heart.

I know from raw personal experience that it is impossible to change oneself by self-will alone—at least any lasting change. Oh, we can vow to "do better" and all that jazz but eventually, well, eventually we find ourselves back to square one because we're altogether human and finite and limited.

But the truth of Scripture penetrating our heart brings about an entirely different result. When we hear and accept the truth of God's Word, it changes our heart—the core of who we are, how we feel, how we act, and what we believe—and when our heart changes, our thoughts change. And when our thoughts change, our actions change. And when our thoughts and our actions change, our words and feelings change. And it is then, my sweet friend, when you see lasting change in yourself and in your family.

So if you rushed through or ignored those important words that I quoted from other people or from the Bible, I want to encourage you to go back and reread their wisdom. You may even want to grab a few of those infamous Post-its and mark two or three of your favorites.

Read through them and ask God to show you a particular verse by which you may find comfort, grace, teaching, and change. Copy it and post it near the places you frequent: kitchen, bathroom, baby's changing station, and minivan. Post it, read it aloud, believe it, and live for yourself the truth it contains.

I hope my own confessions of shared struggles and countless discoveries of hope and change along the way have helped you feel less alone. I am more convinced each year I live, write, and speak with women that hearing and reading the unvarnished truth of someone else's story is paramount to our believing we are not the only ones battling and struggling.

And last but not least, I hope the personalized prayers touched your mothering heart and spirit. I get to do a lot of amazing things and have traveled across the world—literally—but time and time again this consistency remains: I find praying for individuals, one-on-one, undoubtedly to be my favorite thing to do. As you pray, I'd like you to imagine me standing with you—in front of you with my left hand placed on your right shoulder and my right gently pressed against the back of your neck. Our heads bowed—foreheads leaning toward one another—as we simply talk real with God about our needs and His ability to meet them.

That's all.

No fill-in-the-blanks.
No tests or teaching points to ponder.

It's just you and me touching base in the most meaningful and relaxed manner I know. So enjoy, my friend, and know I'm cheering for you from across the miles, cheering and praying peace, joy, contentment, and confidence into your life as a woman and mom. I'll look forward to hearing from you personally as a result of our time together.

Until then!

Julie

Julie Barnhill
julie@juliebarnhill.com
onetoughmothertalk.blogspot.com

Lord,

Thank You for Your faithfulness to each and every one of us.

Thank You for the power of Your Name to heal our deepest hurts.

Thank You for being the Light in the darkest hidden places of our heart and soul.

Thank You for showing up—time and time again.

Thank You for loving us with an everlasting love.

More Mothering Resources

One Tough Mother
It's Time to Step Up and Be the Mom
Julie Barnhill

Visit Julie's blog at
www.onetoughmotherbook.com

Revell
a division of Baker Publishing Group
www.RevellBooks.com

BAKER PUBLISHING GROUP

from Author
Julie Barnhill

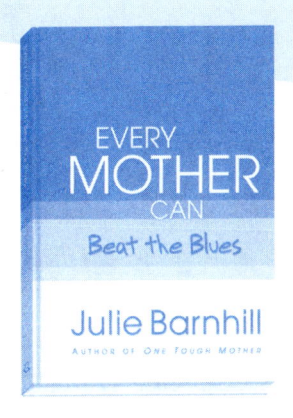

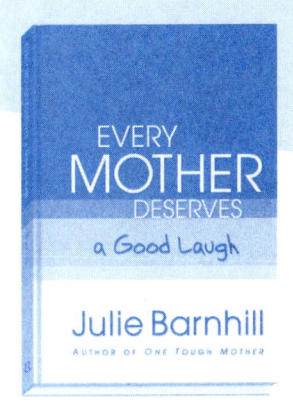

EVERY MOTHER CAN Beat the Blues — Julie Barnhill, AUTHOR OF ONE TOUGH MOTHER

EVERY MOTHER DESERVES a Good Laugh — Julie Barnhill, AUTHOR OF ONE TOUGH MOTHER

EVERY MOTHER CAN Let Go of Stress — Julie Barnhill, AUTHOR OF ONE TOUGH MOTHER

EVERY MOTHER CAN Keep Her Cool — Julie Barnhill, AUTHOR OF ONE TOUGH MOTHER

MOPS
Mothers of Preschoolers

Better together...

MOPS is here to come alongside you during this season of early mothering to give you the support and resources you need to be a great mom.

Get connected today!

MOPS
Mothers of Preschoolers

2370 S. Trenton Way, Denver CO 80231
888.910.MOPS • **www.MOPS.org/bettermoms**